TOP 50 PSYCHICS

TOP **50** PSYCHICS

& Mediums in the U.S.

2016

EDITION

The long awaited list everyone's
been waiting for!

NOW YOU HAVE ACCESS TO THE BEST PSYCHICS
& MEDIUMS THE U.S. HAS TO OFFER

JENNIFUR DIAMOND

Published in the United States of America

ISBN: 978-1519761460
1. Body, Mind & Spirit / Divination / General
2. Body, Mind & Spirit / Channeling & Mediumship

For Maureen "Mickey" Johnson
(September 28, 1944 – May 3, 2012)

Thank you for introducing me to the psychic world.

Bye-bye for now.

Contents

About the Book

The word *psychic* has long been a title given to anyone associated with working in the paranormal. Medium, energy workers, intuitive healer, tarot reader, or any other title these people choose for themselves, the interested client will seek them out by that one word alone, *psychic*. The list of reasons a person may want to explore the avenue of getting a reading can range from finding their soul mate, finances, wanting to contact a loved one or pet that has passed on. Even a skeptic may find they are at a crossroad and are looking for guidance or they just want validation with the direction their life is headed, and the thought of a reading piqued their interest.

Whether you're a believer in psychic phenomena or not, one thing rings true for all of us—"hopefully" at some point in our spiritual growth is a curiosity of wanting to uncover a deeper meaning for which we were meant to travel, and through "psychic" guidance, there can be comfort found, hearing we are not alone in this world.

How can a person determine who they should see when they want to get a reading is by knowing what can be expected by the person giving the reading.

A *psychic* is an individual who has extrasensory perception (ESP) or more commonly referred to as "sixth sense." They are sensitive to things beyond the natural range of perception and are able to foretell past, present, and future events through one's aura relaying pertinent messages to the client. A psychic is able to show the client avenues to go, allowing the client to have an open mind toward new opportunities in their lives that in the past may have seemed out of reach.

A *medium* goes a step further by communicating with the spirit energy that surrounds the client, either by physical channeling in a trancelike state, relaying messages from the spirit world, exhibiting personality traits you may recognize from the deceased or by mental channeling, by using only the mind to telepathically communicate back and forth. With a joining of forces, the medium can then relay messages that come in through ways of not only language but as well as through signs and symbols that have significant and private meanings for the client.

Not all psychics and mediums are alike, and each has their own style of readings. While some do it all, others have an area of expertise. They can use tools to communicate and pick up energy, and some are able to hear clear voices and see clear images, while others have a sense of knowing and can relay the information from that form. To better understand what a psychic or medium may experience during their session with the client, the following list will better help paint that picture:

- Clairvoyant (clear vision) is the ability to clearly see things that are not visible to the naked eye such as spirits, people, places, objects, colors, and/or symbols
- Clairsentience (clear feeling) is the ability to energetically feel the thoughts, feelings, and emotions of what surrounds you.
- Clairempathy (clear emotion) is the ability to clearly experience other people's thoughts, feelings, or emotions as if they were their own.
- Clairtangency (clear touching) is the ability to hold or touch an object, perceiving information about the owner or the history of the item itself, also known as psychometry.
- Clairscent (clear smelling) is the ability to perceive smells and scents without physical origin.
- Clairgustance (clear tasting) is the ability to taste a substance without putting anything in their mouth.
- Channeling is when a person allows their body to be taken over by spirit for the purpose of communicating messages.
- Automatic writing is the process of writing that does not come from the conscious thought of the writer to give messages.
- Remote viewing is a mental ability used by a person to describe and give details about a target or distant location that is inaccessible to normal senses.

A seasoned, legitimate psychic or medium can be an asset to anyone who is privately looking for answers in their lives without turning to family or friends. They are not there to judge you by giving you their opinion on what you should or shouldn't do or how to handle a situation, nor will they give the winning lottery numbers. They will, however, help guide the client and open windows of hope and support if needed as well as show other avenues to explore that are more in alignment with the individual's highest good. The connection made between the client and the psychic or medium can be a learning experience and a positive life-changing event at best.

For all the men and women who have reached out to me, looking to get a reading, all have their own unique personalities that range from the introvert to the extrovert and beyond. In my search for the top fifty psychics, finding those psychics and mediums who could meet the needs of all personality types was my goal. All fifty psychics and mediums bring something new and exciting to the reading with their own gifts and abilities. Whether you're wondering if your new love interest is your soul mate, you're looking to connect with a loved one who has passed on, or you're undecided about taking a new career path, you will be able to connect with one of the top fifty psychics, leaving you feeling clear about the choices that are open to you.

Stacie Bannon

http://www.StacieBannon.com

Stacie Bannon

Stacie Bannon is a full-time psychic and medium out of Nebraska. She is a friendly, engaging, and down-to-earth person who delivers empowering, transformational messages from your spirit guides and departed loved ones. Stacie is the owner of the Holistic Healing Center in Lincoln, Nebraska, where she lives. Stacie does readings locally for clients in the United States and internationally.

After giving thousands of successful readings, Stacie now teaches psychic development classes and performs sold-out mediumship events for large audiences. Stacie has dedicated her life to helping people through the gifts of her intuitive abilities. She's a friendly and down-to-earth person with a good sense of humor that helps to put clients at ease during their reading session. Her style is straightforward and honest; she explains everything to you in ways you can understand.

As one of the best mediums in the Midwest, Stacie connects with your departed loved ones with messages of love, guidance, and comfort to help you find peace. She prides herself on accuracy in receiving recognizable validations and real messages from your loved ones, bringing needed closure for many of her clients.

Stacie was raised in Omaha, Nebraska, through high school. New York City was her home as an adult for thirteen years, so she has a positive, open-minded perspective on life and embraces diversity. Stacie feels very fortunate to have one sweet teenager, a beautiful family, and some great intuitive friends she calls her soul sisters to share this incredible journey with.

Ever since Stacie was very small, she knew that there was "more to life" than what we could see around us because she sometimes would just "know things" she had no way of knowing. She also sees spirits at times. This didn't scare her because she knew that it was natural instinctively. Stacie has other family members who have intuitive abilities or had them while alive, but she is the only practicing psychic medium.

Metaphysics, spirituality, and New Age beliefs have been subjects of great study for Stacie for thirty years. She is college educated, with the strong belief that we should never stop learning, growing, and seeking new perspectives. She loves helping people as a psychic and medium, and also teaching others to open and expand their own psychic abilities. She has a passion for what she feels blessed to do every day.

Clients regularly tell Stacie after reading sessions that they feel much greater clarity about themselves and their lives with a sense of deeper inner peace—even if they receive information they were surprised about. Clients tend to feel lighter, renewed, and truly motivated to move forward with new purpose and positivity in their lives.

Regina Becker

www.Reginas7pillars.com

Regina Becker

At the age of four, Regina was talking to her mother, Hazel, about dreams, premonitions, and making predictions.

Her mother explained to Regina that this started when she had a near-death experience at the age of three and a half and continued. Of course, at that time, the conversation was in child verbiage. Regina's mother became concerned as time went on as these predictions and premonitions were coming true. Thus, Regina was told not to talk to anyone if she "saw or heard" anything that no one else did. Regina went through school being known as a meek and quiet child.

Nursing school, marriage, and children became her priorities for many years, reading only for family and friends. Specializing in geriatrics brought her closer to her mediumship abilities. She was able to give messages to those who felt lost and lonely for those who had passed. This was done in a general conversation way, as she cared for them.

As time moved on, the marriage ended, the four children move on with their families and careers. Regina found that it was time to re-create herself and go into the metaphysical world that she loved full time.

Moving to Green Bay, Wisconsin, to be near her daughter and son and the grandchildren, Regina worked through a crystal store, doing her psychic mediumship, which led to radio, doing the "Monday morning drive to work" for over a year and to guest spots on a Spanish American radio station.

In time, Regina opened her own metaphysical store, which includes a living room so guests can come in and read, chat, laugh, and relax. All are welcome. Regina's 7 Pillars is also the home for psychic medium readings, energy work, and apprentice classes for those who want to expand their knowledge or become professionals in the field. The gift area includes jewelry, rough and tumbled stones, candles, and much more.

Regina continues to encourage all who have this gift to understand and enhance their abilities. Regina is currently writing several books on the subject of the metaphysical realm to help those who seek to understand the happenings in everyday life, past-life regression, and why things go bump in the night.

Marta Berg

marta@Martaberg.com
USA Tel: (310) 421-2252
Brazil Tel: +55 51 9760-0120

Marta Berg

Certified Professional Coactive Coach

Marta has been gifted since childhood, but because she was born into a very traditional Catholic family, she resisted her gifts and ended up first pursuing a career in the technology field. She graduated from the University of Los Angeles, California (UCLA) and explored corporate America. There she realized that was not her true life purpose and began her debut in professional readings (although she had done readings for friends and family for fun, always with happy and accurate results).

Marta has since dedicated twenty-plus years to exploring spirituality and intuitive readings. She is also a certified professional life coach. She impresses her clients with accurate readings as she "picks up energies" and other vibrations. She helps people from all over the world with her detailed predictions. Her card readings usually empower others to move forward, to take action, and to make the best decisions in life. She likes to use the French gypsy cards that famous psychic Marie Anne Lenormand used to read for Napoleon Bonaparte's first wife. Highly intuitive, Marta can impress you with many different spreads for all areas of your life such as love, career, finances, or health.

Down-to-earth and with a very bubbly personality and a cute Portuguese accent, you will certainly enjoy having a read with her

Taylor Brearley

(940) 765-1132

Taylor Brearley

Taylor's evolution into a highly skilled psychic medium and intuitive advisor has been ongoing since his first day. Born with the natural gifts of clairvoyance, clairaudience, and clairsentience, as well as being a highly sensitive empath, his has been a journey of self-discovery through mentoring, coaching, training, and a broad base of life experiences.

Even though he was born with his gifts, he usually says that his true spiritual awakening came in 2005, when at the age of twenty-three he took a life-changing workshop taught by internationally recognized author and psychic Kathleen Tucci. She remains a mentor of his to this day. Within a year of that awakening, he started his own jail ministry, preaching the Word and channeling for inmates.

In 2006 he broadened his horizons and opened his door to clients from around the world while continuing his private studies. His is a profession where there is always more to learn, and he takes his commitment to excellence seriously.

On his journey thus far, he has studied and corresponded with many highly respected professionals around the world regarding psychic work and mediumship, life coaching, meditation, hypnotherapy, spirituality, energy healing and auras, and life paths. One such professional is world-renowned artist on methods of meditation, Alex Grey. Further, he has received his formal certification as a hypnotherapist.

Since 2012, Taylor can say he's conducted over six thousand readings for men and women who come from all over the world and from all walks of life. His natural-born abilities make his reading style refreshingly relaxed and comfortable, while his subsequent studies have honed his abilities to the point where he has a high rate of accuracy. Overall, it is his commitment to honesty and integrity that truly shine through, and this commitment has led many clients to dub him Man of Light.

He looks forward to helping anyone who reaches out in need of guidance and support. As he often likes to say: Confusion Stops Here.

Charley Castex

www.Charleycastex.com
(828) 251-5043

Charley Castex

Charley's unique clairvoyant spiritual counseling is centered on big-picture perspective. Charley's professional focus centers on overcoming challenges, understanding life lessons, and revealing opportunities in our lives. His perpetual goal is to "read for the heart and from the heart."

Perceptually gifted for as long as he can remember, Charley experienced profound spiritual insights at ten years of age and was awkwardly clairvoyant as a young adult. In his late teens, Charley received the gift of mentorship through a four-year apprenticeship with medicine man and author, Sun Bear. In Charley's second decade, he studied psychic development with psychic veteran Joe Nicols, who provided potent inspiration and validation for Charley's empathic sensibilities.

Charley pairs his intuitive gift with his passion for spiritual teaching by presenting intuitive development seminars and inspired spiritual retreats around the world. During his double-decade career as a psychic consultant, Charley has been a key advisor for a multitude of Fortune 500 companies interested in hiring profiles and improving employee relations.

Internationally acclaimed for his clairvoyant accuracy and compassionate guidance, Charley has several high-profile feathers in his cap, having been spotlighted by *The New York Times*, *The Huffington Post* and ABC and NBC national news. Readers of *Mountain Xpress* in Asheville, North Carolina, have consistently voted Charley "Best Psychic" for over a decade. Charley's guidance is a composite of clairvoyance, life direction, and medical intuition. Integrating double-deck card reading and down-to-earth guidance into each psychic session, Charley's visionary gift is geared toward the heart of the matter.

Charley empowers souls globally by phone and provides in-person sessions in Asheville, North Carolina.

Gabbie Chase

Gabbie@guidedperceptions.com
(479) 208-7240
www.Guidedperceptions.com
www.Facebook.com/mediumgabbie

Gabbie Chase

Tinnie, or Gabbie, as she is known (thanks to her granny who insisted that she talked way too much), was born in Louisiana (April 16, 1973) but grew up in the small town of Woodson, Texas. She is a spiritual medium, radio personality, mother, life partner, and teacher. Behind her tender Southern charm lies a story of tragedy and triumph. Within the first seventeen years of her life, she had two near-death experiences and lost her father to pancreatic cancer. Those events brought about a whirl-wind of psychic phenomena that allowed her to strengthen her abilities as a medium and healer, giving her the opportunity to share with others the amazing journey that the spiritual world has to offer.

Her clients have described Gabbie as a friend with wisdom and the gift of peace. Time with Gabbie will open communication to the spirit world and help ease the soul. Her reading style not only will connect you to spirit but help you see the road that can lead you to your spiritual and life goals.

Gabbie has also worked on nationally known missing-person cases and has been a guest on many radio shows. She's also been asked to write a book about her journey as a medium. She is considered an expert in instrumental transcommunication using ITC, EVP, and quantum theories as a means to gather information for sensitive projects.

Gabbie and her partner, Kelli, live in the breathtaking Ozark Mountains near Eureka Springs, Arkansas. They are blessed with two children: Robin (24) and Kerry (22) and their beautiful grandson, Kasin (1). (Gabbie said she can't wait to add to the list of grandkids—the sooner the better!)

She loves her horses and time spent riding on the river. She said it's the best time to revive, rejoice, and rediscover. She is planning to start offering others the opportunity to discover the beauty for themselves by hosting some spiritual retreats in Eureka Springs.

> I am a communicator, a psychic medium,
> and an empath. I try to improve those I encounter. I have the gift
> of communication and empathy, and challenge myself to utilize
> this gift to deliver powerfully effective messages for those who
> seek answers.
>
> —Gabbie

Cheryl "Aurora" Collins

Avalon.biz@gmail.com
(352) 235-0558
Crows Crossroads Shoppe 3810 SE Lake Weir Ave.

Cheryl "Aurora" Collins

Cheryl "Aurora" Collins, named Whitebird by her spiritual elders, started her life in the mountains and ended up by the sea. Her journey took her to Europe, Turkey, Canada, the UK for a short time, and many areas of the United States.

Her spiritual quest began at a young age with hours spent at her grandmother's table, through years of seeking wisdom at various churches, and finding the goddess and nature to be her true spiritual home.

She attended Rutgers University, studied with unity and religious science metaphysical churches, and obtained ordination by the Universal Brotherhood Ministries and Temple of Isis Oasis, Fellowship of ISIS International.

She resides in the woods of North Florida and continues to learn from nature. Aurora has been apprentice to several indigenous teachers and is clairvoyant, clairaudient, and does energy work both near and far. She is a tarot master and has worked with various police departments and Florida search and rescue to successfully locate missing persons.

Aurora has been featured on radio, television, and at several colleges and universities as guest speaker. She has been a professional psychic for almost forty years. You may read about some of her experiences in her forthcoming book, *Whistling Up the Wind*, coming in winter 2015.

Aurora uses psychometry, photos, tarot, and works with your aura. She uses your birth date and the vibrations of your voice as well as the tarot and shaman cards to see your life path and to answer your important questions and share guidance on your past, present, and future. You can change the patterns of your life and create love, beauty, and truth in your life. Aurora can help.

Shelley Dana

(503) 385-5106
www.spiritualblessingsmetaphysicalcenter.com

Shelley Dana

My name is Reverend Shelley Dana. I'm the director of Spiritual Blessings Metaphysical Center. I've been studying metaphysics for over eight years. I started my studies because I was looking for answers to many of life's questions. I have found so many incredible answers and new beginnings. Going through our ministerial program was life changing in so many ways. I have discovered so many new abilities, abilities that I use to help awaken the Divine in all. Besides spiritual counseling, I offer the following:

- *Energy work.* First, I sense and can feel the energy that needs to be released from your aura or body. When my hands hover over the body, I can feel the energy move. I am usually shown images/words with the energy. I work with the angels to pull out any negative energy. The energy sometimes presents itself in different textures, weight, and resistance. Once the body is clear of negative energy, I work with spirit, and the Divine works through me to give you all the healing energy that you need.

- *Light activator.* I call in in the light beings, and they come in as colors, sacred geometry, or other divine images. This energy is very powerful and raises your vibration so that you can accept higher frequencies. As I do this work, I'm able to see past lives. The lives present themselves as images very quickly. I've found that if there is a past life that is affecting this life, this image stays apparent so that a healing can take place. I work with the client after the light activation to talk about the past life that is affecting this life. The client and I work together to help this life heal.

- *Guides and guidance.* Clients come to me as I can see the guides and beings that are around someone. I share who is around you and any messages that they have for you. This helps the client connect in new ways with their guides and how to open up to them.

- *Ghosts and negative forces.* I can see ghosts and other forms of energies that may be affecting you or your home. I can do this remotely via Skype or on the phone. I help release attachments and ghosts that need to find the light.

Veronica Diaz

FB: (Veronica Psychic/Medium)
(310) 684-1446

Veronica Diaz

Veronica has over twenty-five years as a professional psychic. She is clairaudient, clairvoyant, and clairsentient. Veronica has taught classes on astrology and tarot. She also recently published two books, *Hot Advice from a Cool Psychic: How to Get a Great Reading and Not Get Cursed!* and *Hot Advice from a Cool Psychic: On Love and Romance*, available at Amazon.com.

Although tarot is her primary tool for divination, Veronica also reads runes and crystals. She also does energy clearings, guided meditation, numerology, some astrology, and assists people with manifestation rituals.

Veronica has a bachelor of arts in criminal justice and worked for a police department for eleven years. She lives with her family and dog, Odin, in Southern California, where she has a home office. She is also a licensed minister

Karina Duffy

omniloves@gmail.com
www.authenticyou.us

Karina Duffy

Intuitive Psychic Reader and Past Lives / Shamanic Healer / Lifecoach / Certified Counselor / Trauma Release Healer / Somatic Healer / Medium / Crystal and Sound Healer / Animal Healer and Psychic / Relationship and Family Guidance Counselor/ Women Empowerment Coach

Karina was born in Dublin, Ireland, and is from a long line of Celtic intuitive healers and psychics. Her gift of being able to see people's life path and read their aura began as a small child. She assists you in healing by using a method she created called The Authentic Human Journey, which she developed while traveling the world, making a documentary on global connection. "It is about finding your true calling back to your "authentic self." Karina trained with indigenous healers in Africa, India, Polynesia, and the Maori of New Zealand. Karina says, "Living with the indigenous gave me the knowledge of the ancient ways of listening to nature and using its elements to heal the body and mind whilst living life in an authentic way by being true to what is important to you on your path."

When Karina works with you in a healing/reading, she immediately starts connecting with your spirit guides to help bring insightful, heartfelt guidance. She facilitates your healing by tuning into a person's natural energetic current held in the body and restores it to balance with somatic healing, therefore helping to release emotional or physical blockages held in the body, mind, and spirit so an individual can truly live from a place of passion, excitement, and inner knowing.

She is also a trained and certified life coach and is specialized in helping an individual create a map of their lives.

Emalani

www.aheavenlylight.com
(714) 224-6752

Emalani

Emalani is a professional psychic medium who is naturally gifted in working with the spirit world. She is passionate about bringing more love, peace, happiness, connection, and harmony to our world. Her authentic, compassionate, clear, and gentle approach has proven invaluable as she has helped countless of individuals and families work through the grief and healing associated with the loss of their loved ones. Her favorite part of mediumship is experiencing the unique love and connection each spirit shares with the client. She truly believes it is a gift and honor to experience these connections.

Her work also provides help to break negative individual and/or family relational patterns, allowing one to move into a healthier way of living. She also works with families who have a loved one in a coma or those who have nonverbal and or autistic children to bridge gaps in communication. One of her favorite classes teaches parents with autistic children to communicate through telepathy.

She loves teaching a variety of classes such as "Remembering Who You Are." She believes that psychic abilities are a natural part of human life and that we can all learn to access these abilities. Through her course work, she helps her clients to develop their own divine language so that they may see, hear, and feel spirits speaking directly to them.

Through the course of her work, she has had many miraculous experiences, most notably while conducting retreats or giving readings outdoors. She attributes this to the deep, divine connection she shares with nature. As a child it was difficult for her parents to bring her indoors because of her affinity with nature. She believes that God speaks through all things, and her interpretation of what is being conveyed has been said to be a phenomenal experience. She believes that all things are one and that we are powerful beyond measure. To read more about Emalani's experiences, refer to her *Signs of Wonder* blog page.

She has worked successfully on two criminal cases in Southern California and has won many inspiration awards as well as an award for generosity. She has appeared on the *Visions of Inspiration* cable show with Carolina Castorena and *Blog Talk Radio* with Al Diaz.

A certified hypnotist, registered minister, Miracle Center practitioner with training in wise-mind healing using emotional freedom techniques (EFT), vibrational healing, ear coning, and other energy therapies

Rebecca Fisk

www.Iamrebecca.com
(650) 591-1498

Rebecca Fisk

Rebecca is an intuitive psychic who has been sharing her gift to help people for over twenty years. Her journey into the world of psychic phenomenon began when she was twenty-one years old and working as a police dispatcher. It was then that she noticed powerful reactions on her "gut" about people and situations.

Rebecca didn't think too much about those odd feelings; she just thought that her sixth sense was becoming more developed since she worked in law enforcement. A few years later, she went with a friend to see a psychic who told her she had very strong internal guidance and needed to pay attention to it. At that time Rebecca embarked on a spiritual journey by reading books, learning about meditation, the positive effects of prayer, and developing a deeper awareness of energy and how it affects us.

After twenty years of developing her intuitive abilities and offering readings to private clients, Rebecca is now offering her guidance to people, whether it be through her master-compassion workshops or through private sessions for those who seek a deeper understanding of their lives.

Cimi Carol Gates

messagesfromtheangels@outlook.com
(503) 727-5486
15875 SW Boones Ferry Rd Lake Oswego OR 97035

Cimi Carol Gates

Cimi was at home alone reflecting on her day and feeling physically uncomfortable. She recalls sensations of an upset stomach distracting her all day long. Driving home, Cimi noticed feeling pressure in her body just below her rib cage, navel, and pelvic areas.

She decided to go to bed early and began to feel a great pressure in her chest. It seemed like ten strong men pushing her downward. Suddenly, Cimi placed her hands over her heart and silently said to herself, "My God, am I having a heart attack?" To her astonishment, an answer came back loud enough telepathically that she thought someone had come in her home uninvited! There was a very gentle man's voice telling her, "Do not be afraid. We are with you!" Even though this voice was very kind and gentle, Cimi demanded, "Who the hell is with me, and where are you?"

The voice began to explain that there were many angels assisting Cimi in what was called a spontaneous spiritual awakening. Cimi's energy centers (chakras) were opening. Cimi was able to hear the angels (clairaudience) that were present. By the next morning, she could see the angels that were present (clairvoyance), and she could also sense the angels' presence even when they were behind her (clairsentience). By midday, Cimi could go into the future and view events that had not yet happened or go back to past lives to review events for her and others (remote viewing). Cimi's hands became very hot, so hot that the gold on her rings began to melt. Cimi was also able to scan a body and tell where a disease was located and its original cause.

All the events Cimi experienced were happening just as the angels assured her they would. Each of the special gifts came one by one over a twenty-eight-hour period of time. Cimi recalls feeling at total peace as she listened to the angels guide her.

Now these angels truly had their work cut out for them. Cimi not only asked a gazillion questions, she also requested that the angels prove everything to her as they were giving her the information. This adventure proved to be the beginning of a heartfelt healing journey of learning, listening, and loving.

Within a few weeks, the word began to spread among Cimi's friends. People started visiting her for healing sessions, and after several months, she was scheduling healings and readings with corporate executives, foreign diplomats, and airline pilots (to name a few.) Fortune 500 companies and police departments sought Cimi's medical intuition and healing work to help them in their specific fields.

Over the years, the angels have guided Cimi to expand her potential and knowledge of healing and intuitive capabilities. She is happy to share the knowledge and wisdom from these wondrous beings. Perhaps some of these healing tools will inspire your spiritual interest. Just ask the angels.

Cimi had practiced the healing tools the angels had taught her for six to eight months. She was then guided once again by her angels to seek out alternative training that would further validate that information she had been shown years earlier. Cimi's readings include health readings, prenatal readings, angel readings, soul-contract readings, and past-life readings.

Katherine Glass

katherineglass@gmail.com
(978) 987-7289
www.katherineglass.com
FB: Katherine Glass Psychic Medium

Katherine Glass

I'm Katherine Glass. I come from a lineage of psychic sensitive healers and transcendentalists. I am directly related to Ralph Waldo Emerson. I was born in the caul, (also known as the veil), long considered to be a sign of true psychic ability, and I have been using my gifts to bring help and healing to others through my highly referral-based practice for over twenty-one years.

My passion is metaphysics and spirituality, personal growth, and healing. I love the spirit realm and feel very connected to it; the stars, angels, and spirit guides. My family is my heart. I am the mother of two wonderful young men. I love to travel, especially to the UK. I am always learning. I love my clients and feel honored to be a Light worker, serving the planet and spiritual growth here. I am a graduate of the Barbara Brennan School of Healing and Sharon Turner's Awakenings Clairvoyant Program. I have trained at the Arthur Findlay College in Stanstead, England. I give psychic intuitive readings and mediumistic readings in person, by telephone, and on Skype.

I am a gifted psychic medium and energy healer. In my private practice, I specialize in spirit communication, psychic intuitive readings, and energy healing. I use several modalities in my intuitive counseling practice including Brennan Healing Science energy healing, clairvoyance, hypnotherapy, past-life regression, and chakra clearing. I offer group demonstrations of evidential mediumship and readings for families. I am the cofounder of the Healing Essence Center in Concord, Massachusetts, with my husband, healer Jonathan Glass. I also cohost the psychic TV series *6th Sense and Beyond*. I look forward to facilitating personal and spiritual growth on your journey through this wonderful path called life!

Devin Grace

1-800-980-7636
www.devingrace.com

Devin Grace

Psychic Consultant and Master Healer

I am clairvoyant, clairsentient, and clairaudient. I see, feel, and
hear messages from your highest self—the part of you that is
intimately familiar with your life, your lessons, and your healing
needs. During each session I strictly follow the guidance from this
part of you, and the healing begins.

—Devin Grace

For over two decades, Devin Grace, MA has assisted thousands of people around the world to create profound changes in their spiritual, personal, physical, and business lives. As a psychic advisor, master healer, and teacher, her sharp mind, deep focus, and extraordinary psychic abilities cut to the chase and facilitate immediate healing. Devin is extremely versatile and dexterous in her work. She's earned advanced degrees in psychology and business, a master's degree in transpersonal psychology, and has had years of training from some of the greatest teachers and healers in the world. She is an award-winning spiritual screenwriter and published author, a certified depossessionist, and a past-life-regression therapist. Devin serves and is served through her work as the founder and lead practitioner of The Miracle Clinic™, where she offers the many healing technologies she has developed, including

- *Non-invasive surgeries on the physical, mental and emotional body.* During these sessions, the client sees themselves on the surgery table as doctors and nurses bustle around them. Devin scans the body and mind of the client and guides the astral plane doctors as to what may need surgical attention on the physical plane. The client observes as these doctors perform surgeries to remove maladies and restore health.
- *In-depth psychic advising.* During a psychic session, hidden memories, thought systems, and blocked energies are exposed

and released, creating significant, lasting change and enabling a clearer, more powerful relationship with oneself.

- *Spirit-release therapy.* This is one of Devin's most beloved treatments because it not only helps her clients but also assists spirits that are stuck in this plane. Many spirits fail to cross over to the next stage of their evolution at the time of their human deaths, instead attaching to people here on earth. Having a spirit attached to oneself, one's home, or a loved one is not a catastrophe or something to be ashamed of; it is simply an issue that you need help solving. Devin is an absolute master at working with these spirits and has assisted every attached spirit she has encountered in her sessions to make its transition.

- *Advanced Multi-Life Regression™.* These sessions are incredibly powerful for reaching and releasing the origin of issues that are causing problems in one's current life. Devin has developed AMLR™, a method that takes her clients to visit multiple lives and past, present, or future situations that hold the key to unlocking present-day issues. By visiting a series of memories of times when certain fears, phobias, unrequited loves, and hatred of self and/or others originated, the client is assisted to understand the particular purpose these events play in their lives today, enabling direct and immediate healing.

Lisa Greenfield

www.truthinhand.com

Lisa Greenfield

Lisa Greenfield is the founder and CEO of TruthinHand.com. She helps achievers shift unwelcome patterns so they can experience more love and success without endlessly repeating outgrown patterns.

Lisa brings a lifetime of experience, reading well over twenty thousand hands from around the globe. Her readings include iconic film stars, rock stars, international CEOs, television personalities, and people just like you. Lisa has an unparalleled history in hand analysis that brings a rich, deep understanding of human nature reflected in the lines on the hand.

What makes Lisa stand out is her successful career incorporating hand analysis as her secret weapon in the corporate world, where she was rewarded for her sales and management expertise. Lisa received numerous sales awards, including world travel and prizes along with promotions given to her for outstanding results without management ever realizing that her connection with clients and staff was slightly off the beaten path and hard to duplicate.

Lisa's enduring love of peeking into the minds of others started when she was just thirteen years old and her brother used a book from the library to try to read her hand. When Lisa discovered that reading hands was reading minds, seeing the future and still having the choice to change your mind and change the line, she was hooked! She knows it is true; she has seen her own lines change when she took the leap of faith that was reflected in her right hand only to see the line get stronger, deeper, and darker to reflect her change of mind. She discovered long ago that hands are basically the human equivalent of an EEG, providing a fascinating glimpse into a language she was determined to master.

While there was no degree available in her chosen field, she studied it with the same commitment she gave to earning her BA, studying for her MBA, and getting all her licenses for her own stock brokerage firm.

Lisa reads hands everywhere she goes, making her fluent in the language of hand analysis. Her ability is so compelling that upon visiting the set of *Wag the Dog*, Dustin Hoffman briefly delayed filming to have her read several people's hands, including his own and Barry Levinson's, before they returned to shooting. Connecting with people was always a passion for Lisa because of the glimpse of other lives, other stories from around the world, and all walks of life it gave her. This long human chain of hands offers Lisa a perspective rarely found in today's world and inspires a joy in life that helps uplift all those who have a chance to see their best self reflected in a stranger's eyes. It is also what secured her guest spots on radio, network television shows, and awards parties, where her insight into others added value to the program.

It is Lisa's favorite pastime seeing the delight in people who realize that a stranger recognizes their talents and flaws written by their minds in their palms and sees it in the context of thousands of others who survived and even mastered some of the same challenges. A driving force behind Lisa sharing the wisdom of your truth in hand is helping people overcome the common elements of fear and doubt to reconnect with the gifts they are here to contribute.

So when her former employer's identity crisis led to a management change in 2005, Lisa took the leap to start doing hand analysis as a full-time occupation. In order to put the language in the hands of as many people as possible, Lisa wrote a simple software demo to give everyone a free mini sample online. She went on to add an e-book for relationships and a step-by-step guide to teaching you how to unlock your unique life purpose revealed by your fingerprints.

Melissa Hevenor

mhevenor@aol.com
www.Melissahevenor.com
FB: Melissa Hevenor

Melissa Hevenor

Melissa Hevenor is lovingly known as the "psychic in your pocket." Her journey to becoming the "psychic in your pocket" began at the age of four when she had her first encounter with her guardian angel, Robin. By the age of seven she was having regular interactions with the departed and able to see into the future.

Melissa believed that these were everyday experiences for everyone until she realized that she was able to tell her classmates in grade school when there was going to be a pop quiz and others could not. She soon learned that although her abilities were special, they did run in the family. Melissa's great-grandmother was sought after for advice and guidance from the community, in a small rural area outside of Lubbock, Texas. By the time Melissa was born, her grandmother had relocated the family to Washington, DC. Melissa's mother, who also had prophetic abilities, was forced to remain quiet about her experiences. Not wanting Melissa to suffer in the same silence her daughter had, Melissa's grandmother encouraged her to discuss her experiences and express her abilities but keeping them in the family. Therefore, much of her childhood and adolescence, only her closest friends and family knew about her psychic and mediumship abilities.

In an effort to embrace her abilities in an acceptable field, Melissa was quickly drawn to psychology and the arts. She excelled in music and writing, eventually earning a bachelor's degree in psychology as well as a bachelor's degree in theater with emphasis in creative writing. Her joy for helping others compelled her to get a minor in education. She received her bachelors at Florida Atlantic University. Before enrolling in her masters, she decided to reach for the stars in Hollywood, California, landing an internship on the daytime drama *General Hospital*, working in the film editing department. During this time Melissa continued to take screenplay writing workshops and classes. In her spare time, she also wrote commercials for television and special events. To feed her spiritual soul, she took kabbalah courses, and in a short time, she found herself being asked to teach spiritual classes from one of her teachers at the kabbalah center. She began sharing her knowledge with the actors and actresses on set and giving psychic insight. While working on a project in Kinkos, she was approached by a musician who was the keyboard player for Aretha Franklin. Before long, Melissa was helping him build his own brand and assisting him in managing his tour schedule with Aretha. Missing the East Coast, she returned to Florida to further her education, completing her master's degree while working three jobs as a therapist.

Melissa worked with diverse populations including children removed from unfit homes, children on the autism spectrum (as the focus population for her masters in mental health) and with adolescents with addictions /conduct or behavior disorders to complete her second masters in rehabilitation counseling. Melissa loved climbing the ladder in the mental health field and soon became the head of the crisis hotline through the mental health clinic where she was receiving her masters. Melissa felt a longing in her soul to be true to herself and share her psychic gifts. She decided to slowly leave the comfort of the mental health field to embrace her true calling as a spiritual advisor. Melissa was left with no choice but to take the road less traveled when she lost all three of her jobs in the mental health field due to the cutting of funded programs as a result of the economic crisis. Four years later, Melissa has developed a thriving business with clients all over the world, which includes a large fan base in the United States, Australia, and Europe. In August she was asked to host her own radio show on a spiritual Internet radio network. Her show, called *Latte of Heaven*, has a worldwide following. She currently has forty-five thousand followers on Twitter, a full following on her Facebook page, and a loyal fan base on her Facebook fan page as well as over six thousand followers on Instagram and is in the top 10 percent of the business users on LinkedIn. Over the years, Melissa has become known as "the psychic in your pocket" for her willingness to serve as a spiritual teacher to answer common questions asked by the public about spiritual wellness and her experiences as a psychic medium.

There are several skills and characteristics that Melissa has that set her apart from others in the metaphysical field. One of the most unique traits she has is constant contact and communication with her guardian angel named Robin. She does not have to be in a meditative state or prepare in order to connect with the divine. She also has the ability to see the auras (the energy field around people). This ability has been the gateway for Melissa to work with local medical practitioners to help promote wellness and to come up with holistic treatment plans. Having the ability to see auras gives her an advantage when working with addicts in a rehabilitation setting because the aura reveals whatever has been taken into the physical body.

Jorianne

www.coffeepsychic.com
(219) 940-9292

Jorianne

The Coffee Psychic

Jorianne the Coffee Psychic is a nationally known Chicago psychic who has pioneered a new way predicting the future—by looking into a steaming cup of coffee! A variation of the time-honored practice of tea-leaf reading, Jorianne's major form of divination is traditional in Hispanic cultures. Jorianne begins with a quick meditation then pours cream into a cup of steaming coffee. She then receives psychic impressions by interpreting the images she sees in the bubbles, steam, and cream. Over the last thirty years, Jorianne's glimpses into the caffeinated world of the supernatural have accurately predicted marriages, business and artistic success, and personal adventures. "I do psychic readings using a cup of coffee as a crystal ball, seeing images in the steam, cream, and bubbles," says Jorianne. "I see letters, numbers, body parts, faces, images in the coffee. It forms pictures—like a video or motion picture—always moving, always changing. Images come up for interpretation then flow back down into the coffee, and as more cream is added, more pictures resurface for additional information."

Jorianne's psychic talents began to surface when she was a young child of seven, after incurring a head injury. From the ages eleven to eighteen, she lived in a haunted house in Burbank, Illinois, where there were so many paranormal occurrences (such as visions and appliances being inexplicably turned on and off) experienced by her family that they finally conceded defeat and named their resident ghost Sparky.

Not only was Jorianne able to "sense" many out-of-the-ordinary things, but at the age of twenty-one, while cleaning the house one morning, she was visited by "three beautiful nurturing spirits who foretold what was to come that afternoon. They kept saying, 'That's right, that's right, clean up the house for the funeral tonight.' I heard the voices three times, once each consecutive hour. That afternoon my mother died suddenly," she remembers. "That experience left me feeling confused over what I experienced and why. I decided to investigate the paranormal to find out why I could hear and see things that others could not and what to do with this gift.

"My connection to reading coffee psychically began early in my paranormal explorations," says Jorianne. "I was discussing different methods of divination with my sister-in-law's cousin, who is Hispanic, and she introduced me to the use of reading coffee this way, which is traditional in Hispanic cultures. Being a coffeeholic myself, this seemed a natural for me and was my first attempt at learning how to access information psychically.

Jorianne studied psychology at Chicago's Richard J. Daley College, receiving her associates of arts degree, moved onto GSU in Illinois, majoring in psychology. Jorianne became a certified hypnotherapist and Reiki healer. She is a member of the Association for Research and Enlightenment, the Edgar Cayce–based foundation. She is also a certified Universal Light minister and has, over the last thirty years, been featured on radio and TV shows. Jorianne has also hosted her own radio show for the last ten years.

Lori Karras

1-888-813-2277
www.Talkpsychic.com

Lori Karras

Lori has over twenty years working professionally in the psychic field. She began as a much-sought-after tarot reader and intuitive astrologer to eventually becoming one of the best-known names in the psychic media industry. Lori has hosted and provided psychic readings for radio and television. She has helped many a celebrity client connect with just the right reader for their needs. From TV productions to infomercials to personal readings to building a network of quality psychics, Lori has just about seen and done it all, especially on the professional level.

When first developing Talk Communications and www.talkpsychic. com, it was because psychic companies wanted (and needed) someone who had the psychic ability and was intuitive and talented enough to review potential readers who was also capable of managing a large group of mystical specialists to ensure there was *always* a quality reader available to clients twenty-four hours a day, seven days a week. Though others were considered, her clients knew she was the one they wanted to assist. You too will discover Lori's talent from her down-to-earth, straight-to-the-point readings!

Once you start utilizing her or her company's services, you will quickly discover why clients send her psychic calls to answer and also, if you are lucky enough, to have her give you a reading.

Clients keep returning over and over because Lori and her staff really do strive to provide genuine psychics and readers and readings for your personal needs, and Lori is a big part of that success!

Scott Keith

scottkeith@icloud.com
(949) 716-2810
www.scottkeith.com
FB: Scott Keith Psychic Medium

Scott Keith

Scott Keith is a gifted psychic, medium, and spiritual advisor who has been providing answers and insight to his clients for over twenty years. His easygoing approach is welcoming to his clients from all walks of life. Scott likes to refer to himself as your "one-stop psychic shop" as his unique abilities cover many different spiritual areas. Relationships (both personal and professional), your life path, health concerns, connecting to loved ones who have passed over, and even questions about pets and real estate—Scott can provide answers in all these areas and more.

Originally from Philadelphia, Scott followed his heart to Los Angeles and now currently resides in Palm Springs, California. Scott loves to travel. Whether embracing the spiritual magic of the Hawaiian Islands or the rich history of old Europe, he naturally connects with energies wherever he goes. On request, Scott has traveled to meet with clients in various parts of the country to look at real estate and to give in-person readings. However, Scott does most of his work over the phone from his home office, realizing that his clients are most receptive to receiving their spiritual information from the comfort of their own home wherever they reside on the globe.

Most clients want to know about relationships, whether it be regarding a partner, sibling, coworker—you name it. Working with his clients' own spirit guides, Scott interprets their messages, providing guidance and peace of mind. As a medium, connecting with a loved one who has passed on often gives his clients healing and an understanding into things that were perhaps left unsaid.

As an animal advocate, Scott takes great pleasure in connecting spiritually with animals. Sometimes we just want to know what our furry friends are feeling, both emotionally and physically.

Finding your life's work and career path can be difficult without guidance, and sometimes we can all benefit from an outsider's perspective. Scott finds your passions and can steer you in the right direction when it comes to a fulfilling career and a life path that's right for you.

Scott believes that we all could use help at times, and he truly loves to be a part of lifting someone's mind, body, and spirit. With his down-to-earth demeanor, Scott has built a loyal client base and assures complete confidentiality.

Above all, Scott's approach to life is to live in abundance and unending happiness. Working with Scott can bring you clarity, peace of mind, and answers to life's most important questions!

Harriette Knight

www.HarrietteKnight.com
661-254-4747

Harriette Knight

As a child, Harriette Knight experienced vivid past-life memories of Nazi Germany, believed that those who had passed away watched over their loved ones, and, as early as fourteen years old, fixed up couples according to their astrological sign.

"I've always loved anything metaphysical," she confesses. However, if anyone had told Harriette that she would become a respected healer and psychic medium as an adult, she wouldn't have believed it. Her passions were art and writing, and through many career changes and professions, Harriette finally surrendered to her first love, metaphysics, and has been in practice ever since.

Harriette is a master healer, psychic medium, spiritual guide, and author, and has recorded over two hundred broadcasts for her radio show *Harriette Knight's Psychic & Healing Hour* on Blog Talk Radio.

Among Harriette's accomplishments, her books *CHAKRA POWER! How to Fire Up Your Energy Centers to Live a Fuller Life*, and *GEMSTONE POWER! 52 Meanings and Meditations from Abalone to Zircon*, along with her guided-meditations CDs, have become a staple for those on a spiritual and metaphysical path. Helping to bring metaphysics to the mainstream, she has appeared on television, in *Women's World Magazine*, and has done live readings on numerous radio shows.

Everything Harriette does comes under the banner of healing. Her purpose is to support others to become the best that they can be by letting go of old patterns, moving forward in life, and finding peace of mind. A perpetual student as well as teacher, Harriette is well versed in psychic phenomena, mediumship, past lives and reincarnation, animal totems, astrology, oracles, healing modalities including Reiki, prebirth planning, chakras, gemstones, and more. "You never know what will come up during a healing or reading," she says, "but it is always what the client most needs to support his or her journey."

Harriette transitioned to reconnective healing in 2001. Reconnective healing goes where it most needs to go on all levels—physical, emotional, mental, and spiritual. Throughout a healing session, done in person or distantly, Harriette receives detailed psychic messages specifically for the client. Whether it is a message from a loved one or a certain age or lifetime to be released, the information is very helpful, loving, and healing. Harriette is a motivating speaker who has helped to enlighten others about numerous topics including astrology, past lives, and how to reclaim their personal power. Her enthusiastic and uplifting spirit has helped clients all over the world. She lives in the Los Angeles area and is available for life-changing psychic readings and healing sessions by visiting *www.HarrietteKnight.com*.

Sarah Lambert

http://BodyInsights.com

Sarah Lambert

Sarah Lambert started as a massage therapist before having a dramatic and unexpected psychic awakening in January 2009. Lifelong abilities to channel, read energy, and do profound physical and energetic healing work that had been mostly dormant until that time suddenly came forward.

Over a two-week period, she lost her ability to eat or sleep and had a series of intense visions about humanity's role on earth, the overall message being that each person is seeded with a unique gift or life purpose, the sharing of which evolves the individual and heals the planet.

The awakening left her more conscious of her own gifts and her ability to help each person name and fully express his or her purpose, yet at a loss regarding the practicalities of running a business and translating her visions into reality. So she sought teachers who could help her better understand and apply her work.

These included awakened teachers and masters of internal martial arts, who taught her to focus entirely on how energy works and to be exceedingly practical in her application of ideas. To her surprise and deep, personal transformation, they taught her not to channel and to focus solely on showing up fully and effectively in her life. She learned through working with them that intuition works best when we focus on the details and "ordinary" aspects of life. This builds a strong container that can then handle the full force of our highest potential.

The result is her psychic readings are about much more than helping clients clarify their situation. She does active healing and coaching that taps into exactly where and how people are caught in their journey toward self-realization and their best and most reasonable steps according to their situation to achieve what they want in life. Her readings are unique to the needs of the individual and do not rely on formulas but rather speak to the specific situation of each person, suggesting practices based on her reading of what will serve them best.

Her readings are unique in that they combine with bodywork. When she does a reading on an issue in someone's life, she sees exactly where and how it lives in their body and what's needed for it to shift physically as well as mentally. The result is healing work that actively moves energy in the session, so lifelong problems are noticeably shifted, and the body feels profoundly better.

Eve

info@elitetarot.com
347-87-TAROT (347-878-2768)
www.elitetarot.com

Eve

Elite Tarot

Eve at Elite Tarot specializes in using tarot to help executives and business professionals navigate career options, personal dilemmas, and business-strategy decisions. Her approach is straightforward and empathic, with a touch of lightheartedness and humor.

Eve's path to tarot was an indirect one. Intuitive since birth, Eve has been providing insight for decades to those at crossroads. This has taken the form of personal matchmaking for single professionals, crisis intervention with police response units, and outreach to those dealing with terminal illness. With tarot, Eve has found the ideal mode of expression for her unique approach to intuitive coaching.

Eve's readings are positive, optimistic, and empowering. She sees herself not as a predictor of specific events but rather as an intuitive coach with all the power remaining in the clients' hands. She helps them unlock the answers inside themselves regarding life paths they are taking, choices they are making, and decisions they are considering. In Eve's hands, there is nothing scary about a tarot-card reading as it serves only as an aid to help clients achieve optimal happiness and success.

With an education and background in business, Eve is skilled in working with business professionals and organizational leaders. Eve has helped guide professionals at all levels, from lawyers to CEOs, small-business owners to nonprofit advocates.

With clients from Los Angeles to London, Tanzania to Seattle, Eve at Elite Tarot has helped people worldwide gain clarity and insight with professional tarot-card readings. In-person readings are conducted in the Washington, DC area, while phone and Skype readings are available worldwide.

Each of Eve's readings comes with a recording of the entire session, a summary sheet of everything discussed, and a photo of the final tarot card layout.

Educated in part overseas in England, Eve has a master of business administration (MBA), and she is certified as a tarot-card reader by the Tarot Certification Board of America. She is a member of the American Tarot Association, Tarot Professionals (UK), Tarot Association of the British Isles, and the Capital Tarot Society.

Adrienne Lynn

www.consult2achieve.com

Adrienne Lynn

Adrienne Lynn's intuitive strengths coupled with her strong affinity for the runes empowers her to inspire, motivate, and uplift those she works with, enabling them to gain perspective, resolve their issues, obtain their objectives, and make satisfying progress in all aspects of their lives. She speaks the language of the heart with focus, empathy, and clarity. Her ability to read the energetic dynamic of the issues that affect her client's lives, well-being, and happiness, whatever the issues or situations may be, enhances the insight, guidance, and information she imparts.

The scope of topics Adrienne Lynn reads on are as broad and complex as life itself. Family and friends first evidenced Adrienne Lynn's psychic abilities and spiritual awareness during her early childhood, most notably through her mediumistic experiences, energetic connections, and profound metaphysical and spiritual inquisitiveness. As she transited into adulthood, she placed her focus on acquiring greater spiritual knowledge and mastering the full range of her psychic talents as an intuitive, clairaudient, clairvoyant, empath, and clairsentient. She sought out, studied, and successfully worked with various tools, until 1987 when happenstance led her to the runes. The energetic connection was so immediate and magnetic that the challenge of acquiring the ability to communicate with an oracular medium, in its own language, became one that was mastered rapidly. The connection fully opened her to intuiting the complex fluid dynamic contained within each of the twenty-four runic symbols and the nuances of the blank rune. Innately, her personal psychic language understood the runes' mystical one. Wondrous and awe-inspiring, the runes instilled a great reverence within Adrienne Lynn. The highly refined, well-targeted introspective approach to the matter at hand, the strikingly natural mode of expression, the underlying psychological insight and philosophical perspective, and the uniquely oracular guidance the runes provided made it quite clear they were the perfect match to her own natural psychic approach, insight, and perspective. Delighted to have found a supremely optimal medium for the outflow of her psychic talent, her innate comprehension of the human psyche, and her keen intellect, she began using them, exclusively and without delay, in her work with her clients.

The runes remain the only tool Adrienne Lynn will use to assist her. As her powerful gravitation to the runes as her complimentary reading tool was strongly influenced by her own psychic flow and perspective, her reading style is strongly influenced by her strength of personality and character.

The profoundly compassionate, genuinely concerned, immensely kind, insightfully intelligent, nonjudgmental, sincere, and straightforward delivery evidenced in all her readings is a clear reflection of inner nature. She inspires, motivates, and encourages her clients as she intuits the answers they seek, the resolutions they need, and the new options and alternatives open to them in addressing the issues, circumstances, and relationships that are currently too difficult to for them to handle or continue on with. Her natural creativity harmonizes with her psychic ability, strengthening her power to look at old problems in new ways and enhancing the tools and techniques she provides to further support her clients as they navigate out of the negative into the positive.

During the course of her consultations, she draws deeply on her inherent psychic strengths, her natural affinity for working with diverse energies, and the wisdom of the oracular runes. Always she does so with an open heart and an open mind, and always with great intent and a singular focus finely filtered to penetrate each client's personal situation and needs. Perceiving life as progressive and ever changing, that we are energetic beings with the option to exercise free will, that very little in life is unalterable and that there are always options and alternatives, Adrienne Lynn's natural optimism shines through, adding an uplifting spirit to her readings.

It is Adrienne Lynn's unwavering belief that we all can, with the right perspective, guidance, and insight, determine right solutions to problems, make decisions with clarity to achieve the progress we strive for and truly create and live the quality of life we desire. From the strength of this belief aligned with her deeply rooted spirituality and warmhearted dedication to assisting others, Adrienne Lynn found her calling: to support as many as possible as they journey through life by nurturing their evolution and providing them the guidance they need to successfully navigate their paths. Hence, her mission is to enable her clients to grow and excel inwardly and outwardly, acquire wisdom and tools to deal with life issues, gain a sense of empowerment, find peace and serenity, and come to a place of happiness and contentment. In doing so, she finds purpose and enjoys a smiling heart.

A native of New York City, Adrienne Lynn has been happily fulfilling her mission, globally working with clients through private appointments, consultations by telephone, Skype and other live webcam venues, and by providing videotaped readings in response to presubmitted questions. Clients from widely varying backgrounds, in incredibly diverse circumstances, confronting an infinite range of issues generated by the ebb and flow of their lives have all continuously benefited from sessions with Adrienne Lynn.

In keeping with her natural affinity for working with energy, Adrienne Lynn is a certified Reiki master practitioner in the Usui tradition. Her professional Reiki practice enables her to alleviate emotional, physical, psychological, and spiritual conditions, further fulfilling her mission to well support others through their life journeys. She also engages in the study and practice of qigong, augmenting her insightful connection to and beneficial use of universal life force energy. Her educational background includes a BA degree in the dual majors of English literature and education from York College of the City University of New York, followed by a MA degree in English literature from New York University. As a published photographer and an artist, her work has been exhibited and is in private collections in the US, the UK, and Italy.

Adrienne Lynn's dynamic intellect, spirit, and creativity enhance her innate psychic ability to perceive the diverse energies that influence all our lives. This heightened proficiency well serves her clients in receiving the specific counsel they seek.

Adrienne Lynn can be contacted through her website: www.consult2achieve.com.

Jeff McBride

www.jeffmcbridereadings.com
860-483-0096

Jeff McBride

Jeff is an internationally known and tested reader with over fifty years of connecting. He is a born psychic medium, the author of *Living in 2 Worlds*, a certified Reiki master, and a former police officer. Being a natural-born psychic medium, there are no tools required to obtain your information.

He connects quickly to those who have past and provides evidence of whom it is being contacted. All energies are available—relationships, business, lost items, pets, and much more. Distant viewing, energy healing, and life coaching are all part of what is offered in your reading—great readings for a reasonable fee.

Jeff McBride is a natural-born psychic medium who has spent his life listening and seeing. Energies from the past, present, and future are available to him, and he connects quickly to those who have passed on. Jeff's paranormal awareness and psychic abilities have been interlaced with everything he has done. As an actor and model for over thirty-five years, Jeff has appeared in several national ad campaigns, films, and TV shows. Jeff is the author of *Living In 2 Worlds*, his personal memoir about growing as a clairvoyant child and how he used his gifts to create a successful life.

We are all born with a specific gift. For me it is the ability to live in the physical world while maintaining constant communication with the spiritual world. This is how I was born. Since early childhood, I've been able to see and talk with spirits. Through my adolescence, I turned to these people at times for assistance in my decision making. As I matured, my ability increased, and my trust grew stronger with every success that I was guided to. Through time I learned I could use this ability for the well-being of others. I offer you this site as an alternative source of information that can be used for your personal progress. This information could come from a past relative, a future event, or a change of mind-set that will lead you to your answers. Take a look around and see what what's available to you!

Eve McGann

(352) 245-5275
evemcgann@embarq.mail.com

Eve McGann

Eve McGann, known as the Angel Reader, is clairvoyant, clairaudient, and clairsentient, and is an empath. Eve has been in metaphysics since the age of twelve when her spiritual talents became obvious.

Eve was instrumental in the awakening and fostering the talents of Bill Clark, nationally known spiritual healer and channel. She is included in the book about his life, *Do You Believe in Signs?* by Shalomi.

She studied with Noel Street and William Swygard, accomplished spiritual healers, as well as being in Unity. Eve is ordained through the Universal Spiritual Association of America, in Chesterfield, Indiana.

Eve will channel for you angelic messages concerning your past, present, and future. She includes people, places, and things to assist you to plan and improve your life.

Eve teaches how to make your dreams come true. She will answer any question that you may have at the end of the reading, if they are not already answered.

She has read for clients throughout the US and Central America for over forty years; she can help you get answers.

Rhonda Manning

Rhonda@PsychicMediumRhonda.com
(901) 324-2586
2010 ExeterRd Suite 2 Germantown TN 38138

Rhonda Manning

Rhonda Manning is an internationally renowned psychic medium and one of the top psychic mediums in the United States. Not only is she an incredible evidentiary psychic medium (scientifically tested and shown to have a 90 percent accuracy rating) but she is also a trained psychotherapist in private practice for over eighteen years. To bridge the gap between science and spirit, Rhonda routinely serves as a guest speaker at paranormal institutes, radio shows, and holistic and spiritual expos across the country. Because of her ability to explain the scientific aspects of intuition, she is able to give lectures on everything from mediumship and the science of intuition to quantum physics and the energy body.

Another factor that sets Rhonda apart is how she came into her psychic abilities. She was suddenly gifted in her late thirties in what she describes as a profound spiritual experience from God. She then trained with shamans, mystics, indigenous medicine people, and other mediums in order to develop her skills. This journey has led her to an understanding that we are incredible energetic beings living in a galaxy within multiple universes all made up of energetic frequencies.

Her popular audience readings, called Speaking to Heaven galleries, are inspiring testimonials to life on the other side. Her ability to speak to loved ones who have crossed over is even more impressive because during communication, she can "direct dial," meaning that she can contact specific spirits people wish to speak with.

Life path readings. Rhonda does private readings by phone or in person. She does in-depth soul readings that describe past lives, the soul's purpose, personal guides, and chosen life lessons, as well as answering general life questions. During the reading process, Rhonda can even remote-view places and people half a world away as though they were in the same room!

Medium readings. Rhonda contacts loved ones who have crossed over to heaven. Her descriptions of the way they died, the number of family members, their physical appearance, and other personal details clearly validate that there is a true connection to your loved one. At times she even takes on mannerisms of loved ones in such a way that confirms their presence.

Other services. Rhonda lectures, gives classes, and does mentoring in person or via Skype. She also presents small-group readings in private homes in Memphis, Tennessee, and the surrounding area. She is available for travel and lectures.

Lois T. Martin

www.loistmartin.com
(518) 989-6349

Lois T. Martin

Psychic Numerologist

Lois is a practicing psychic numerologist with years of experience, and in her words, "The numbers speak to and through me. Being given one's name and date of birth, I hone into a "psychic in high definition" (PHD) mode, pencil and paper not necessary, where voices, tones, shapes of letters and numbers from higher realms are clearly clairaudient "heard" for messaging."

People reference Lois as not only the Hot Number Lady but a highly respected spirit communicator/medium. She is very active in public appearances, tutorial programs, and private sessions by appointment.

Aleta Mason

www.HonestPhoneReading.com
Home office between 9:00 a.m. and 8:00 p.m.,
US mountain time (505) 610-3342
Backup/emergency number, cell (505) 573-7964

Aleta Mason

Aleta L. Mason of Psychic Readings & Healing is a professional psychic and energy healer in Albuquerque, New Mexico, USA. She provides readings worldwide by phone and e-mail as well as readings and healing in person, at her home office, and at her office in Nob Hill, Albuquerque.

She was born into a family of psychics and artists and grew up in the suburbs of New Jersey. Her intuitive and healing gifts were quickly recognized and encouraged by her family from a very young age. Her gifts have "morphed" over time but started out with such things as telepathy, psychokinesis (aka telekinesis), including healing people and repairing electronic items simply by touching them, precognition/clairvoyance, angel visitations, dematerialization/teleportation/out-of-body experiences, and more. One of the most memorable experiences was an angel visitation during which she was informed of her purpose in this lifetime; she was told that she was here to help and support others.

There were always library books in her house on various metaphysical topics, and her education in these matters started as a child. Her formal education/training started in her early twenties (in the mideighties), and included classes and workshops in psychic development, Reiki, aromatherapy, herbalism, and more. She has since used this training to help many clients gain clarity, closure, guidance, and healing. Being an earth sign and very "grounded," her readings are down-to-earth, practical, and to the point.

She was guided by very clear dreams and signs, starting in her teens, to move to New Mexico, the Land of Enchantment. Her readings provide insights and understanding of people, relationships, and situations. Clients present to her a wide variety of questions and issues such as relationships, career, money, relocation, pets, and more. She calls upon the ancestors, guides, and all spirit helpers of the client and utilizes the tarot cards to confirm her impressions. She reveals the motives and characters of people, the quality and potential of relationships, and advice to improve these relationships. She helps people choose the best career, location, romantic partners, and offers advice regarding "unexplained phenomena" in their homes as well as holistic consultations for health improvement. Her clients get more than predictions; they get solutions and advice that help them onto the path to their best future.

You will find that her readings are very affordable. Her primary motivation and passion is to be of service and to be accessible to all.

John Michael

sessions@johnmichaelpr.com
www.JohnMichaelPR.com

John Michael

John Michael has been in the metaphysical industry now for close to thirty years and has been an established psychic/astrologer on many levels for over close to three decades. He began his career quite by accident at a very early age, when he began having vivid dreams about planes. He would write down his detailed dreams and not only identified the plane but also captured the tail number. This finally caught the attention of his maternal grandmother, whom he confided in, who was also psychic, and many of the planes he dreamed of were eventually involved in tragic accidents. Even though he aspired to become a lawyer, his "gifts" sealed his fate. And as fate would have it, his reputation of accuracy in his readings grew. Since that time, he has devoted all his energies in becoming the very best at his craft and also affording his clients with the most affordable readings in the industry. His clients today are like the "who's who" in today's society. They range from housewives to some of the most influential people in today's headlines. Because of the confidentiality that most of his clients require, a strong and enduring security system has been established to ensure confidentiality with all private readings that are conducted on a secured line. John Michael employs two mediums with all his readings.

Having spent well over twenty years studying astrology, he uses astrology only as a template to coordinate all his readings. What makes John Michael's readings most appealing to his clients is that they can interject questions to him at any time during the one hour reading, and he explains the astrology associated in his readings in terms that the client understands. Most of John Michael's established clients have been with John Michael for well over ten years.

His credentials are far too many to mention here; however, here are just a few: Graduate, Colorado University at Boulder, Colorado; MBA Graduate, Boston University, Boston, Massachusetts; JD Psychic Readers Network (PRN) 1995–1998; contributing astrological writer for *OMNI* magazine 1996–1998; featured, Keen Network Astrologer/Psychic 2009–2014; cofounder of United Society of Metaphysical Counselors.

John Michael established his own business providing personal readings for his "family of clients" in June 1996 because of the high demand for his services while still keeping a very hectic schedule on various psychic networks. Due to the expanded growth of his personal business, he retired from the psychic network industry in May 2014 to solely provide and concentrate on private readings for his personal clients. He insists that he wants to make his readings available to the masses no matter their income. That is why his fees have never changed. As John Michael best describes his services, "Everyone has a situation in their lives at one point that requires more than just a friend, lover, or family member to turn to for sound and unprejudiced advice, to turn their lives into the equation of what they want their lives to be." This mantra is what makes his readings so desirable.

Lisa M. Miller

www.LisaMillerPsychicMedium.com

Lisa M. Miller

Lisa M. Miller is a spiritual psychic medium, animal communicator, and healing practitioner with over twenty-five years of experience. As a child she could hear electricity, see colored "energy" dots that could be manipulated into shapes, and telepathically communicate with her pet birds. If there was any doubt about being a medium, it was shattered while walking through Gettysburg's Wheat Field, allowing a deeper connection in spirit to the soldiers' physical pains, heightened sensations of their presence, and reliving their despair. The most influential experience in her development occurred when the presence of a civil-war spy merged energies with Lisa. Her friend was startled by the physical transformation on her face and in her body gestures, and to this day, Lisa considers this experience her psychic boot camp.

Blending her gifts of clairvoyance, clairaudience, and clairsentience with her ability to work in the shamanic realms, Lisa may delve deeper into the physical, emotional, and spiritual aspects of the soul to bring insight, guidance, and healing into areas that are perceived obstacles to moving forward. Her down-to-earth style embraces compassion, honesty, validity, accuracy, ethics, and often, humor, as cited by over three hundred testimonials shared by her clients.

Lisa earned both a bachelor's and master's degree in metaphysical sciences from the University of Metaphysical Sciences and is currently working on her doctorate in mediumship. She is certified in soul retrieval, shamanic, and Usui Reiki, crystal light color balancing, and axiatonal alignment.

Lisa has been featured on local cable and radio as well as national psychic radio talk shows. Her dedication to helping others has allowed her to work with some of the top paranormal investigators in the field as well as assist in missing children, missing pets, and unsolved criminal cases. She offers private and group readings in her office as well as public mediumship galleries in the tristate area.

Lisa M. Miller resides in Honey Brook, Pennsylvania, with Fred, her husband of twenty-five years, and her two pet birds, Rio and Cacao, often featured on her website and Facebook page.

Ann Marie O'Dell

www.Thecallingoflight.com
http://achieveradio.com/ann-marie/

Ann Marie O'Dell

Ann Marie O'Dell is a certified national intuitive reader with forty-plus years of psychic reading experience. She belongs to two National Psychic Reading sites, is an esteemed member of Best Psychic Directory, reads privately by phone, Skype, and at her garden studio, and has over twenty-eight thousand national client reviews on her accuracy. Private sessions can be scheduled through her website, www.thecallingoflight.com. Also a published spiritual author with Balboa, Ann Marie's book *Gardens of the Sisterhood*, sold through Barnes and Nobles and Amazon, is an exploration on creating magical gardens with metaphysical tools, statuary, wind chimes, and feng shui.

How It All Began

Ann Marie's earliest childhood memories were orb-filled dreams, faces looking intently at her that disappeared in air, and classrooms in which the extra layer of "seeing" and "feeling" the energy of the children around her became more interesting than what the teacher was saying. In the 1970s, at age nineteen, Ann Marie discovered a beautiful deck of cards called tarot in a French gift shop. Fascinated by the symbolic art, through the cards, she realized her true gift of psychic reading. As the rhythm of the cards clicked like drums in her hands, she went into a deep meditation, which she refers to as connecting with her angels. Her answers to client questions resonated with such accuracy, and her journey of professional psychic reading began. In the early years, she read at college art fairs and gift shops, which expanded to phone readings in 1999. Told that her voice is soothing, Ann Marie has found a second home with Internet Psychic Radio, where a larger audience can tune in and hear her gift as well as meet novel spiritual guests that drop by.

How She Reads

Ann Marie believes the mark of true psychic accuracy is in receiving a reading on your now before asking for information on an unproven future and asks for only a first name, telling all she "sees" around her client's present life. If what the seeker hears rings true, a connection has been established. From here Ann Marie takes questions, always following the code of certified ethical reading and relaying tough information with in-depth strategy and honest compassion.

Ann Marie says, "The beauty of intuition is that on turning fifty, a beautiful calm set in, and my psychic gift soared as clarity became magnified. I feel more deeply connected to my angels than ever before."

*The Calling of Light *Achieve Radio

Jack Olmeda

(516) 568-1829
Olm4@optonline.net

Jack Olmeda

Psychic Clairvoyant, Palm Reader

As a young boy, Jack would have vivid, lucid dreams about the people whom he knew. "When I told people about the dreams, they were amazed because what I would dream would eventually happen to them," says Jack, who grew up in Queens and the Bronx. Jack found that he had a talent to tap into the psychic world as well as the ability to channel spirits of the deceased. While a teenager, Jack worked as a "trance medium," channeling the spirits of the people who had passed away and giving information to their relatives. "After each reading, I felt very tired and drained," says Jack. "I just couldn't do it anymore." Jack took a break from psychic work, until he ended up in the hospital with a collapsed lung. Jack says that his "spirit guides" came through during the illness and told him that he must "follow the path" of helping people through his psychic gifts.

Jack says that he now conducts psychic readings using tarot cards as well as palm reading. "I tend to read very quickly because the information is being channeled so quickly," says Jack. "I encourage people to tape the sessions." Jack also conducts healing sessions with a Reiki master and reflexologist. Jack uses his psychic vision to guide the two healers to areas of the client's body that need healing energy. "A reading helps a person to control their destiny," says Jack. "When I predict that a negative event will occur, the client has the power to prevent his event. God gave us free will so that we can all change our destinies."

Melissa Peil

melissa@mysticalawakenings.com
(919) 621-5912
www.mysticalawakenings.com

Melissa Peil

I have been psychic and intuitive since birth and have had many spiritual experiences throughout my life. In 2005 I truly awoke to my spiritual gifts, and my psychic talents were sparked by the death of my grandfather. His passing was the second time I was aware a family member died before anyone else knew. I was inspired to learn more about what had been happening throughout my life. I began connecting with other like-minded individuals who were navigating on their own spiritual journeys and read as many related books I could get my hands on. I took a few classes that gave me the tools to enhance my natural gifts, which allowed me to take off and fly. Even today, my gifts continue to evolve and shift as I grow and change. I am grateful every day to do what I love and love what I do. I teach adults and children alike about their intuitive gifts and guide many through their fear of the unknown gifts they are unlocking. I am a teacher by trade, having earned my bachelor's and master's degrees in education. I taught elementary school for a few years before fully stepping into my path as a full-time psychic medium. During this transition, I became aware of the need to combine my passion for teaching with psychic mediumship work to help those who need to understand what they're experiencing and reassure them they're not going crazy!

In 2010 I contributed to the book *Kids Who See Ghosts: How to Guide Them Through Fear*. I shared my experience running a support group for families with intuitive children through www.meetup.com. The group offered insight as to what intuitive children may experience and how I could support children with these gifts and experiences and their families. On my website I offer a survey for parents to use with their child to gain a better understanding of what their gifts are and the level of their psychic development. When I work with a new student, this survey provides me with a starting point so I can tailor our sessions to specifically meet their individual needs. Thanks to the Internet, I am able to work with children anywhere who need my assistance. To further my spiritual development, I received training in Reiki 1 and 2 in 2014. This was prompted after feeling energy coming through my hands during a number of sessions with clients. I am now able to offer Reiki energy healing to clients during sessions as their needs arise. I have completed training in past-life regression therapy in 2015 and am excited to add this to my toolbox.

Originally I'm from Rochester, New York, but follow my intuition as to where I call home. In the past I've lived in Raleigh, North Carolina; Seattle, Washington; and currently reside in Boston, Massachusetts.

Vessa Rinehart Phillips

mokitup@san.rr.com
(858) 509-7582

Vessa Rinehart Phillips

At the age of six, Vessa began communicating telepathically with animals. In 1984, at the age of nineteen, while attending UC Berkeley, she entered a clairvoyant training program at an institute in Northern California and was later hired on as a staff member. For the next fourteen years, she trained others to develop their own psychic abilities. In the spring of 1997, she appeared in video productions with renowned psychic Uri Geller and fire-walking instructor Jon Cotton.

Vessa later earned a master's degree in management of nonprofit organizations and has served as treasurer for the Berkeley Area Interfaith Council. She is an ordained minister and for many years was the pastor of a metaphysical nondenominational Christian church. She has had her own television series, *The Intuitive Insight & Alternative Healing Show*, and has been a popular guest on Los Angeles radio talk shows.

Vessa also presented intuition workshops and healing seminars in major cities across the country, including Atlanta, Boise, Philadelphia, and Seattle, and has authored numerous articles in New Age publications. Today, Vessa is director of Intuitive Insights—an organization dedicated to teaching people to develop their own intuition and clairvoyance.

Donna Pinter

donna@donnapinter.com

Donna Pinter

Donna is an internationally renowned artist. In addition, she is a born intuitive counselor, medium, and channeler and has work with clients for over thirty years. In 1984, Donna's life took a miraculous turn when she was given the advice of a rough and tumbled carpenter who took part in building her artist loft. First, she witnessed an expeditious healing of an injury that occurred to the carpenter while on the job. His finger had been severely cut. However, when he returned to her home the next day, his finger was completely healed without any medical attention. During the course of this same day, he happened to show a liking to a blue angel in the sky from one of Donna's paintings. She was dumbfounded as the angel was not a conscious intention. This gentle, calm man advised her to trust that help was always there for her. When the day was over, they said their good-byes. However, she never saw this gentleman again. Donna knew this message was delivered by an angel. Her fate was sealed.

Donna channels a collective group of angels called the Blue Ray Healers. Along with the ascended masters, the blue rays are dedicated to supporting the shift of humanity into higher levels of consciousness. Donna's beloved teacher and mentor, Ethel Lombardi, was among the first five Reiki master in the US as well as the channel for the MariEL healing and now joins her often from the other side as she works. Aside from being a Reiki and MariEL master healer, Donna uses many other healing modalities in her work. Hypnotherapy and past-life regression has led her to a unique way of clearing issue back generationally as well as past incarnations as to end the cycle in one's DNA codes and karmic patterns forever. Rebirthing, holographic healing, the success and healing codes along with many other techniques to help her get to the heart/root of the issue once and for all in record time.

Donna Pinter is a nationally and internationally exhibited artist with well over two hundred solo exhibitions in galleries as well as museums. She is in the process of completing a new interactive website dedicated the angel support messengers that have gone around the world in the past two years along with online classes and conference calls. Along with all this, she still finds time to create community mosaic projects involving the help of children through the public and private school system. Donna is truly a visionary. Her list of publications, featured articles, TV and radio guest appearances is impressive, including National PM magazine; TV feature, ninety minutes, Tokyo, Japan; arts southwest; Atlanta & Philadelphia, Angel Times, Art and Spirit magazines; Dr. Ilene Benner blog talk radio; Dr. Joanne White on *Power Your life* radio; the Guild Sourcebook Interiors and Architecture IV, XII, XII, X11, XIIII; *Who's Who in American Art* and *Who's Who in Psychic Atlanta*, which Donna also designed the cover art for the book. Donna has also written two children's books about angel spiritual awakening along with a book of poetry and art called *One Voice* in collaboration with Dan Lis.

Donna is now dedicated to teaching and mentoring the next generation of spiritual leaders. She is happily married and lives in Atlanta with her husband and two furry rescue four-legged boys.

Eliza Rey

elizarey@cox.net
(480) 861-0840
P.O. Box 25275 Scottsdale, AZ 85255

Eliza Rey

Eliza has been performing readings for over twenty years. She has touched the lives of many with the intuitive messages from our guides, including past loved ones.

Eliza has experienced intuitive abilities since she was a very young child and was able to visualize and hear messages for and from her family. A tragic accident occurred when she was eighteen years old involving the deaths of her brother and father, which motivated Eliza to further develop more of a connection with those on the other side.

Since then, Eliza has helped others connect with past loved ones, providing loving intentions and counsel for others. She has assisted others with concerns and questions regarding family, relationships, work and health concerns, and has helped others in making more intuitive life choices. Eliza also is a writer, occupational therapist, and mother of two.

Eliza is available for speaking on her program *Intuitive Tools 4 Kids* as well as consultations on developing your intuitive gifts.

Debby Ritter

debbie@eclipse.net
(360) 504-2398

Debby Ritter

I knew from an early age I was sensitive, and for much of my life, I wished it were otherwise. I took my intuition for granted and used it to chart a life that was nonlinear and marked by fresh starts.

Out of high school, I spent a year in Aix-en-Provence and some memorable years on Cape Cod. Later I buckled down academically and got a degree in Mandarin Chinese. That led to ten years spent living and working in China. On my return to the States, I commenced a long period of caring for my parents. Despite the challenges, being with them in their last years was one of the great, heart-opening joys of my life. During that time I also went to law school and subsequently practiced environmental law for five years.

Throughout, I was a dedicated spiritual seeker, studying and practicing yoga, Buddhism, and many other teachings, including A Course in Miracles and the work of Byron Katie.

In recent years I have relocated to the Olympic Peninsula in Washington State. Living here in such natural beauty feels sacred and has helped me develop my spiritual awareness and also acknowledges my psychic abilities. I work primarily in the Akashic records and have been certified by Linda Howe's Institute for Akashic studies through the advanced teaching level. An Akashic record reading is similar to a psychic reading, but the information comes from the perspective of the soul. In addition to readings, I teach others to read their own records, and I am also a medium, tarot reader, and spiritual mentor. My intention is always to provide a safe and compassionate space for clients and support them as together we allow the wisdom and clarity of their highest selves to shine through.

Virginiarose

www.theppa.net

Virginiarose

Renowned house whisperer, medium, and spirit liaison, Virginiarose recalls interacting with the spirit world as early as two years of age. After many years developing and fine-tuning her ability, Virginiarose began professionally assisting clients with her mediumship abilities. Virginiarose has over thirty years of professional experience as a psychic medium and continues to help people with her work.

Virginiarose lectures on metaphysical topics around the country. She has taught metaphysical subjects in public school adult education programs for over seven years and meditation classes for over twenty years.

Virginiarose first began working with the PPA in 2009, providing metaphysical information to the team during investigations. She identifies potential sources and causation of hauntings and provides guidance through the resolution stage of the cases to help bring closure for the clients.

Known as the House Whisperer, Virginiarose has appeared with the PPA on numerous episodes of the television series *The Haunted*.

She is currently working closely with the development executives at Face OFF Productions on numerous projects in various stages of production.

Kerry Ryan

www.kerryr.com
(208) 830-3434

Kerry Ryan

One of the joys of my work as a psychic medium is observing how Spirit meets each client exactly where they are with compassion, patience, and respect. One client may be seeking evidence of the afterlife, and his loved one in spirit bring it through, while another may want to understand her eternal path and purpose, and a past life may come through to illuminate it. Continually, I learn from Spirit that divine love is without judgment, without condition. Through spiritual connection we can learn much about our true selves, much about divine love and the nature of our amazing, energetic, multidimensional cosmic existence.

The opening of my psychic medium abilities followed the sudden and tragic death of my oldest son, Kevin. Just thirty-six hours after he passed, his spirit came to me in an "after-death visit," which is much like a near-death experience—an experience of the reality of the afterlife that often changes the one experiencing it forever. It has changed my life, the way I think, and the way I am. Knowing the reality of our energetic existence and that Kevin's spirit continues in connection with my own has helped me through my grief and heartache. Just five months after Kevin's spiritual visit, I began giving readings professionally. To pass forward to others the comfort and peace of connecting with their loved ones in spirit and continuing in relationship with them is a great joy.

The heart of my work is connecting my clients with the healing and transforming love and power of Spirit. Whether this power is coming through in a private reading, a group reading, or a healing series of readings, it reaches out, touches souls, and transforms. To come to love ourselves and see ourselves as the Divine does is what the spiritual journey is all about. To connect with spirit and communicate with spirit and work with our spiritual guidance can help us see ourselves through the unconditional love of the Divine and to treat ourselves with loving-kindness. With this kindness we are transformed, empowered, and able to let go and be present to the moment and to whatever is in our lives.

I offer readings in person in the Boise, Idaho, area and by phone or Skype to anywhere else on the globe. If you would like to learn more about my work, the readings, and the services I offer, you can visit my website.

Lorry Salluzzi

lorrysalluzzi@gmail.com
(516) 708-5213 text or call
www.psychic-healter.tv
Red Hook and Lanesville, near Phoenicia

Lorry Salluzzi

Lorry Salluzzi sensei found Reiki in 1990 when her sister was diagnosed with terminal Hodgkin and non-Hodgkin lymphoma. Lorry had already been battling with terminal systemic lupus after she lost her entire family to a terminal disease. She was diagnosed in 1988 with systemic lupus. She had heart and lung involvement, skin lesions, and was crippled for two and a half years. Her medications: Procardia, Plaquenil, and prednisone, were keeping her alive but not making much difference in her quality of life. When her sister's life was threatened with terminal cancer, they decided to do something drastic. They looked into the things their other family members did not—the psychic and holistic world of healing.

First came guided-imagery meditation. As soon as she started it, her med's dosages went down. Next came the discovery of Reiki. Lorry used Reiki on herself and helped her sister as often as possible with Reiki. Both Lorry and her sister went into remission and remain in remission today! This was the reason Lorry got involved with Reiki.

Not only did the practice of hands-on healing energy medicine and guided imagery help her to achieve remission, but they helped her to tune into her psychic clairvoyant abilities. She realized that she was always a natural medium. Lorry effortlessly sees energy: the aura, the energy within the body, and most times the spirit world that is always around us.

Lorry sometimes uses tarot and angel cards to access answers for her clients. Her sessions are accurate and therapeutic. Most clients leave her feeling great hope, feeling relaxed and healed on some level.

She has been a psychic and Reiki teacher since 1991. Lorry founded the 11:11 Soma Healing Center, lectured at major book stores regularly, appeared on several radio and television shows, teaches at Ulster County Community College, is part of the Merrick Health and Wellness Center on Long Island, Body Central in Red Hook, Mirabai of Woodstock, New Beginnings Spa and Salon in Lake Katrine, Izlind Health & Wellness of Rhinebeck, the Salluzzi Center of Sebastopol, and more. She has taught hundreds of thousands of people Reiki and psychic development. Her students are among the most successful psychic practitioners and you can find them all over the globe.

You can read her story as one of the main characters in the book *A Circle of Quiet: Two Sisters, Two Diseases, Two Remissions* by Rhodes and Farley.

Available for private readings and workshops in Red Hook and Lanesville, near Phoenicia.

Kathryn Schiff

www.kathrynschiff.com

Kathryn Schiff

Kathryn was born and raised in Dallas and educated in Virginia and Paris. She lived in San Francisco most of her adult life where she was a partner in a successful commercial photography agency. A free spirit and adventurer, she has traveled to many places in the world, exploring, searching, and listening. During a long stay in Buenos Aires, something shifted in her intuitive space. She started noticing messages from the universe, what many would see as coincidences or strange occurrences. These were very personal and direct. The more she opened her eyes to see, the more information arrived.

Soon she moved to Santa Fe, New Mexico, and started meditating. Almost immediately her sense of self shifted. She had discovered a language that spoke to her—a silent language. After several years of study at The Center for Inner Truth in Santa Fe, developing her sixth chakra, she became a clairvoyant reader, certified as a teacher of intuition, and ordained as a spiritual minister.

Today, Kathryn practices a unique method that psychically looks at the client in terms of growth cycles and life path. She does a healing on the energy centers, or chakras, and clears one's personal psychic space, or aura. This helps to release energetic stagnation, other people's energy, fear, and other emotions that keep one from healing and from moving forward. This process of letting go allows more clarity and ease in one's life path. Kathryn works together with the client to create a healing, and she also clairvoyantly reads what is going on.

Life is limitless. This experience creates a shift in some way, whether small or large. Learning to let go of one's "stories" enables a positive experience of connecting with one's true self. If one is religious or atheist, it makes no difference. This is an experience of the self, whatever your true self is.

Kathryn offers guidance with taking the next step forward in life. She helps the client bring more joy into life. Her readings involve getting messages from the spirit world, the departed, loved ones, and guides. She looks at specific questions and helps the client to manifest and bring more into their lives. She offers help with illness and pain, healing relationships, cutting cords and agreements. She looks at past lives. Clients learn to form better boundaries. Kathryn does pet healings and works with animals. She also offers house and business clearings. Her goal is to help her clients create more space, clarity, peace, and healing so that they can live more fully on their authentic path. If the client is an advanced healer or practitioner, or unaware of this quality, she helps to work with any confusion that may create. Kathryn teaches clairvoyant and energy-tools classes weekly, privately, and with the Intuitive Insights Center, Los Angeles. She does this work in person and over the phone.

Jenni Sinclair

www.jennisinclair.com
(503) 332-8224
(657) 212-5303

Jenni Sinclair

Jenni Sinclair began recognizing her abilities at the age of twelve and has since devoted her life to revealing and refining her psychic abilities and spiritual awareness. She combines her intuition with tarot, numerology, and astrology to provide accurate and informative readings. Her highest purpose is to help others gain inner peace, greater confidence, and greater self-esteem. Her readings offer accurate information concerning relationships, money, career, health and family. By illuminating your life path, Jenni helps guide you to your true destiny.

She is also a ThetaHealing© Practitioner, a process that empowers others to remove and replace negative emotions, feelings, and thoughts with positive, beneficial ones. ThetaHealing® can be most easily described as an attainable miracle for your life. In addition, she is a recognized law of attraction advanced practitioner certified by the Global Sciences Foundation. Her ongoing search to deepen her consciousness and expand her spirituality has also led her to extensive training classes through the Centers of Spiritual Living and to become a recognized Joe Rei Healing Practitioner through the Izonome Association.

Featured on various television and radio programs, Jenni has created a presence and following of clients worldwide. Whether on the radio, television, at psychic fairs, exclusive in-home parties for corporate and private clients and those in the entertainment industry, Jenni consistently astounds believers and skeptics alike with her extraordinary, accurate, and upbeat readings.

She is coauthor of *Gateways to Change*, a numerology book that offers an upbeat perspective to keep your bearings as you navigate through life's challenges.

Currently Jenni lives in Santa Ana, California, with her husband Don, their two dogs, Keanna and Buttons, and their cat, Coco Kitty.

Jethro Smith

psychicjethro@aol.com
(928) 284-0437
www.jethrosmith.net
FB: www.facebook.com/psychicjethro
Twitter: https://twitter.com/psychicjethro

Jethro Smith

Jethro Smith, part Blackfoot Native American Indian, was born with the gift of sight and the ability to see auras around people. Extraordinarily gifted, his abilities became public at an early age and heightened after a near-death experience. Jethro was intensely tested and trained by metaphysical masters beginning preschool, continuing throughout his twenties. In kindergarten he began foreseeing future events and communicating with his classmates' loved ones who had crossed over.

Today, Jethro's longest-running clients are his friends from elementary school. "We went to school together, and as my prophecies came true, I went on to read for their husbands and wives, whom I had predicted, and to also read for their children, whom I had predicted."

Serving professionally as a psychic intuitive and investigator for over thirty years, Psychic Jethro is known for swift, concise, and powerfully accurate spiritual readings. Jethro works only "in the light" to help others in their spiritual path. He is the proud father and grandfather of two sons and two grandsons.

He has written two books:

- *Uncle Jethro's Guide to the Sixth Sense: Awakening Your Intuition*

  What if your natural gifts were heightened to a level beyond your imagination? What was once a gut feeling can become an extremely heightened sense of clarity. Uncle Jethro's guide book provides step-by-step instruction and fascinating true life experiences to help you understand and develop your own natural intuition.

- *Living in the Psychic Realm*

  The unique true-life story of innocence, spirituality, and psychic development. Likened to "a real-life Harry Potter," Jethro's story chronicles nurturing one's gift to "do good" in a world of choices between dark and light. Simple yet eye-opening, the tale explains psychic development for all age groups and opens the imagination for developing one's own intuitive gifts.

Jethro is a certified psychic, certified tarot reader, certified Reiki master, reverend, and author.

Countess Starella

(772) 468-4681
www.countessnadiastarella.com

Countess Starella

Countess Starella is the flamboyant clairvoyant. A magical mystical queen of the elementals, her bold presentation and regalia will capture you with laughter and fantasy.

Here are profound messages wrapped up in mirth from one of the psychic world's most colorful characters. This is a benevolent soul walking the path of a master. She is versed in psychology, philosophy, metaphysics, science, religion, theater, music, costuming, and much more.

Through extensive study and world travels, Starella has created a system to bring forth the most favorable atmosphere in which you may achieve and manifest your dreams. Her simple, easy-to-implement techniques have enriched the lives of over 175,000 clients worldwide. By practicing her own methods she has managed to live an exemplary life with no doctors, enough energy to work twenty hours a day, seven days a week for twenty-two years, and a joyful, positive demeanor unequalled.

Once you have connected to such a mystic, you are able to claim your greatest power, self-love, and true destiny. Starella brings a rare and precious love and counsel to this planet.

Doug Tessler

https://www.facebook.com/doug.tessler?pnref=lhc
(561) 715-8544

Doug Tessler

Doug Tessler has been called a seventh-plane saint and a musical intuitive.

He is a mystical and ethereal guru and counselor, offering messages and sacred sound healing for creating bliss and clarity in your life.

He has the uncanny ability, as a musical savant, to not only counsel you but play any kind of music you may need for vibrational healing.

Doug plays a plethora of musical instruments, from the indigenous didgeridoo to sacred ancient woodwinds and flutes, the finest and most diverse music of the angels, saints, and spheres.

This biographer ventures to say that no one alive can make you feel more loved and in harmony with the universe than Doug.

In a lifetime, only a few living masters appear, and to find one with the humility and devotion required to keep one's balance in the material world is a miracle; and Doug Tessler is one such miracle

His many thousands of devotees worldwide will attest to the magic and magnificence he brings to one's life—offering insightful clairvoyant information to help those struggling find the answers they need in their lives to be successful, happy, and to feel fulfilled.

Once you have experienced the warm, nurturing love that Doug will embrace you in, you will retain his services for the rest of your life.

His wife, Doc Simm Gottesman, acupuncture physician, has been creating healing music with Doug, using an angel harp, and together they are helping people heal through ancient and modern techniques from qigong to herbs and diet.

Thomas Thunderhoof

tozororion@yahoo.com
www.tozororion.com

Thomas Thunderhoof

I have been a shamanic practitioner professionally for seventeen years. Since I was a child, my connection with Spirit was always strong, and I have always felt I was a part of something bigger. I was led to Arizona where the lessons I learned were a journey of the soul where Life, Death, and Rebirth, along with Shadow work and the shamans' death prepared me for the work that I now perform. Though I need no tools, I do use the Sacred Path Cards by Jamie Sams and the Medicine Cards by Jamie Sams and David Carson.

Through meditation, ritual, and ceremony do I keep connected to my spirit guides and power totems. I am a seer, teacher, healer, and warrior. I will release my clients of any disturbance that they may have troubling them and give them knowledge to help follow up. I will get to the root cause of your problem and give sound answers to any and all questions that arise. My abilities enable me to correct and heal mind, body, and spirit. To free you of confusion and give you Spirit-led messages that pertain to the direct situation, I use a personal medicine drum to heal and reconnect all to the heartbeat and rhythm of mother earth. There are no problems too small nor any that are too great that cannot be solved as the love and light of Spirit is channeled through me to give you guidance, direction, health, wealth, and welfare. My goal is that you may be blessed as you walk this earth in beauty. Alo!

RayNelle Williams

raynellew@gmail.com
805-216-2881
www.Raynelle.com

RayNelle Williams

Intuitive Numerologist, Soul Reader

Since 1999 RayNelle has been reading numbers for clients around the globe. After twenty years in successful corporate careers, she resigned to dedicate her life to sharing her gifts to help others gain clarity in their lives.

A reading with RayNelle can change your life! Known for her amazing accuracy where clients often ask, "How did you know that?" or "Are you inside my head right now?" She can't make this stuff up; it comes from your unique numbers.

RayNelle intuits soul readings through the numbers in your birth date and birth name. She describes it like this: "When you go to the ATM to withdraw cash, you first have to input your four-digit pin code. For me, your numbers are like the pin code to your soul, which gives me all entry access to your energy." A soul reading with RayNelle gives specific details. She answers questions about you, your relationships, career, moves, decisions you need to make, and more.

A recent testimonial: "Authentic, the real deal. RayNelle never met me before last night, yet, she was able to tap into the very depths of my being. I asked for nothing, yet she gave me a road map that was clearly defined and one I recognized as mine. She explained to me about strengths I came into the world with, the destiny I was seeking, and how to balance the two. That's when she gave me the road map—how to get there."

What can one do when you're face-to-face with a person who's channeling a higher power and the information she's giving you is just for you? I'll tell you what happened to me. My jaw dropped. I realized RayNelle is real. And then I listened. She's the one you're looking for. Believe me when I say I was seeking the answer to a question I didn't know. She opened to the universe, and the information came through her. Her energy is beautiful, loving, and honest."

Mary Beth Wrenn

marybeth@marybethwrenn.com
(704) 566-8300
www.Marybethwrenn.com
FB: PsychichMaryBeth

Mary Beth Wrenn

Mary Beth Wrenn is a natural psychic medium who sees auras. Your life is a direct reflection of your heart's projection. Your aura projects your thoughts, holds your soul's past lives' memories, and carries your internal and external images into the future. Your soul knows the future. It's the ego that decides as to which direction to take. We all have free will, and we each have the capacity of making impactful decisions based on intuitive knowledge that we receive.

Mary Beth will predict your future by accessing the energy field of your aura, in combination with the esoteric knowledge of the tarot, empowering you through important experiences in your life. She's going into her thirtieth year as a professional psychic medium.

Leigh Cohen Wyatt

(763) 684-1453
www.leighcohenwyatt.com

Leigh Cohen Wyatt

Leigh Cohen Wyatt is a certified professional intuitive, relationship, and psychic life coach, empowerment expert and healing facilitator; clairaudient, tarot-reading, voice-recognition psychic. She is also a gifted clairvoyant, certified chakra balance instructor, and medium who teaches people to move forward with compassion and grace.

She teaches her clients how to uncover their own personal power and life potential. Leigh is a nationally recognized psychic featured in many magazines, directories, and has hosted many radio shows. Currently Leigh is the owner of the Best Minnesota Psychics directory. Leigh provides a road map for her clients in understanding that the journey is not just about the outcome but the process to achieve your desire.

About the Author

Jennifur Diamond has spent a lifetime devoted to her spiritual and psychic gifts. The work she has done has comforted others when they have lost loved ones and opened windows of hope for those who thought they were lost. While Jennifur's gift is not one that she expected, she has acknowledged that it is what she is meant to do and shares her talent in every way that can help others. As people continued to turn to her for psychic guidance, it became the motivating element to promote other psychic and mediums with those same gifts and abilities. This culminated into the creation of the *Top 50 Psychics*. Jennifur lives in Beverly Hills, California, and is founder and contributing editor for an online publication, www.psychicsuniverse.com, and is author of the book *Waking up Psychic*.

Made in the USA
Middletown, DE
23 December 2015